SHOSTAKOVICH

CONCERTO No. 1

in E♭ major, Opus 107

FOR CELLO AND PIANO

(MSTISLAV ROSTROPOVICH)

Published in 2019 by Allegro Editions

Concerto No. 1 for Cello and Piano
ISBN: 978-1-9748-9971-5 (paperback)

Cover design by Kaitlyn Whitaker

Cover image: "Cello" by Mindscape Studio, courtesy of Shutterstock;
"Black and White Piano Keys" by Nerthuz, courtesy of iStock;
"Music Sheet" by danielo, courtesy of Shutterstock

ALLEGRO
EDITIONS

CONCERTO No. 1
in E♭ major for Cello and Orchestra, Opus 107

Edited by MSTISLAV ROSTROPOVICH

I.

DMITRI SHOSTAKOVICH
(1906-1975)

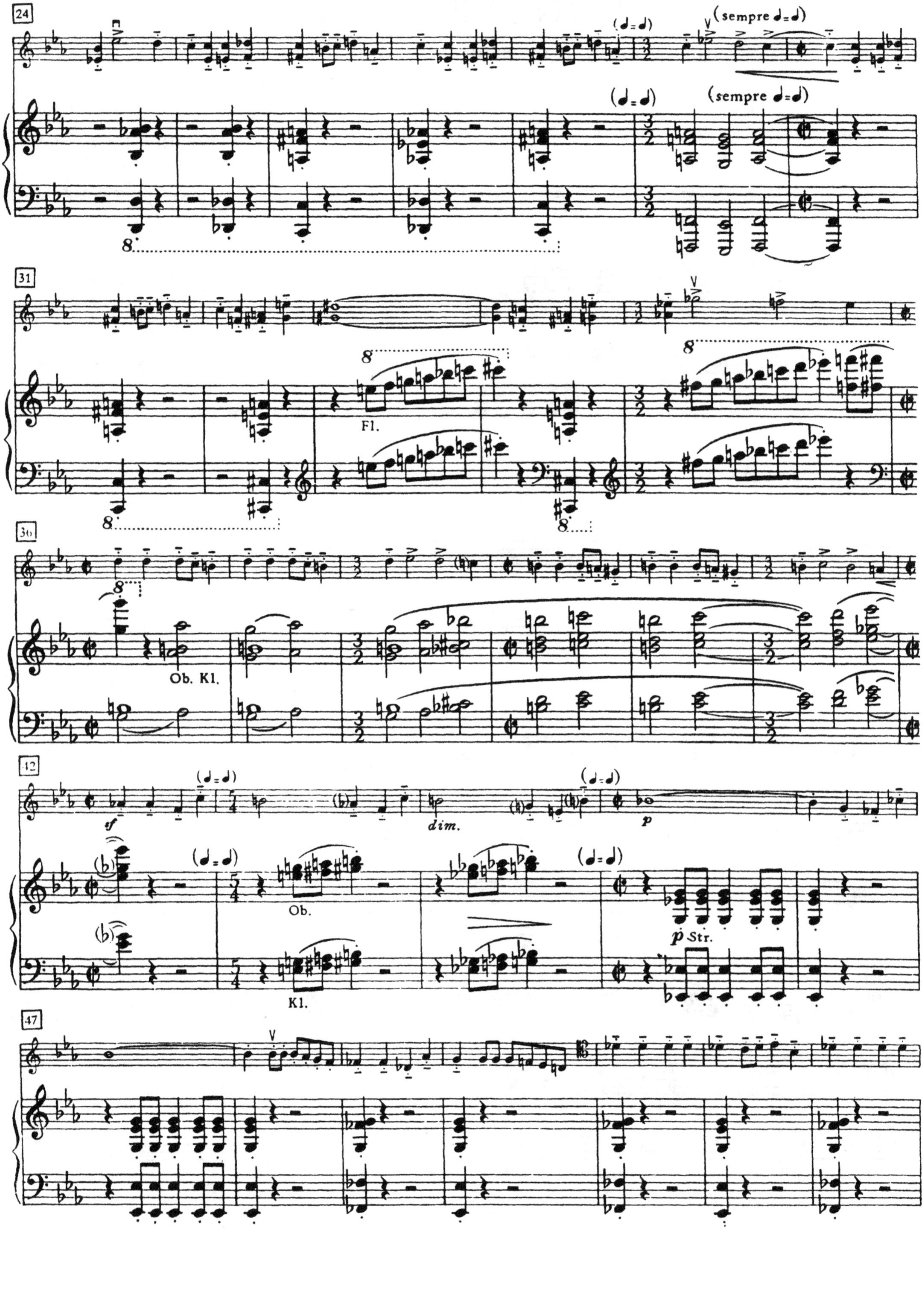
24
(sempre ♩=♩)
31
Fl.
36
Ob. Kl.
42
dim.
Ob.
Kl.
p Str.
47

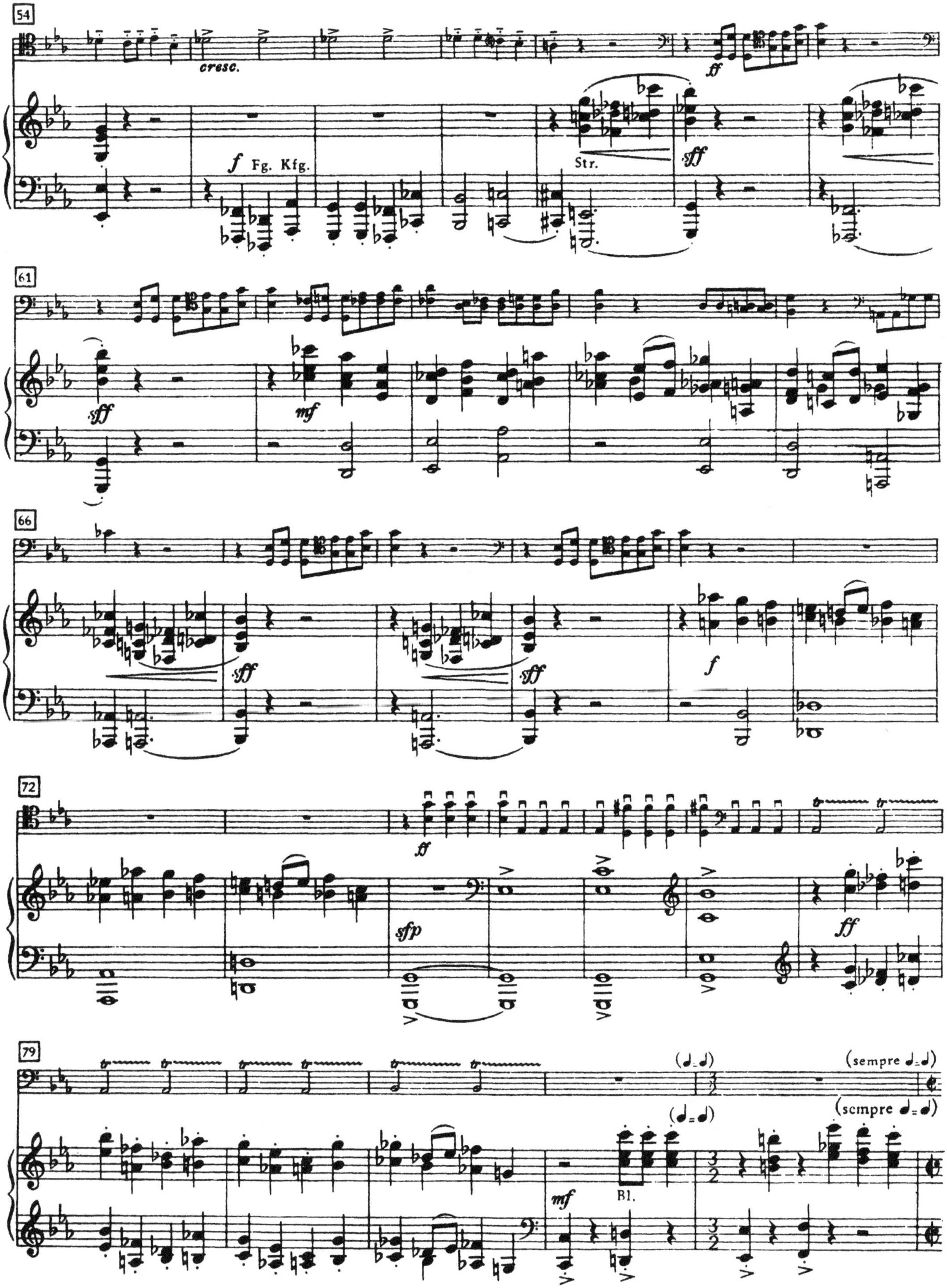
54
cresc.
f Fg. Kfg.
Str.
61
66
72
79
Bl.
(sempre ♩=♩)

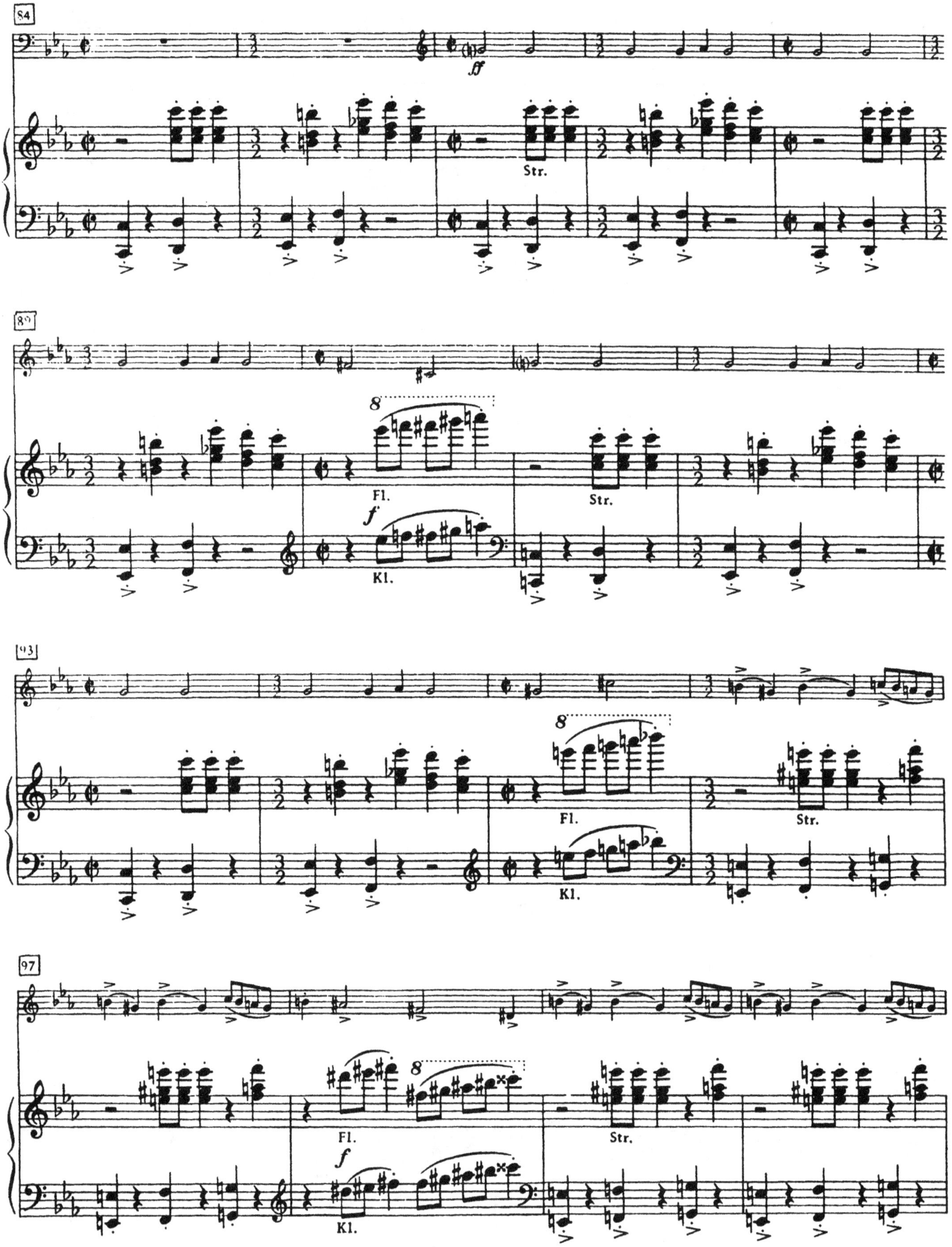
84
ff
Str.
89
8
Fl.
f
Kl.
Str.
93
8
Fl.
Kl.
Str.
97
8
Fl.
f
Kl.
Str.

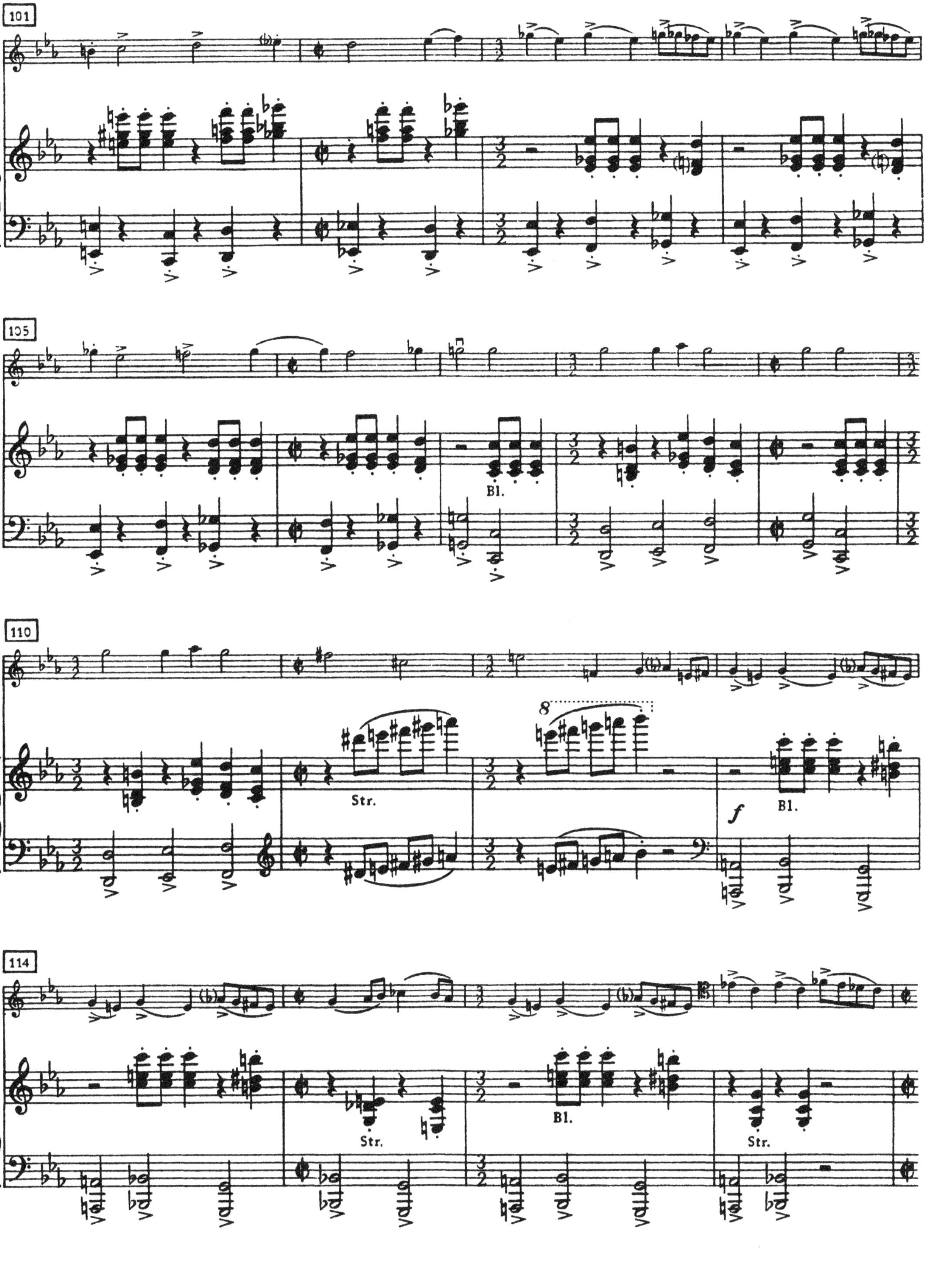
101
105
Bl.
110
Str.
8
f
Bl.
114
Str.
Bl.
Str.

118
dim.
f
mf
dim.
123
dim.
Va.
dim.
Kl.
p
mf
Vc.
127
132
cresc.
Hrn.
mf
mp
Str.
138
f
p
ff
p Str.

146
dim.
p
ff
f Fg.
Kl.
p Kl. Fg.
Kfg.
154
f
dim.
p
Str.(pizz.)
159
ff
f Ob. Kl.
8
164
Fl. Kl.
Str.
Fl. Kl.
169
Fg.
Hrn.
f
Str.

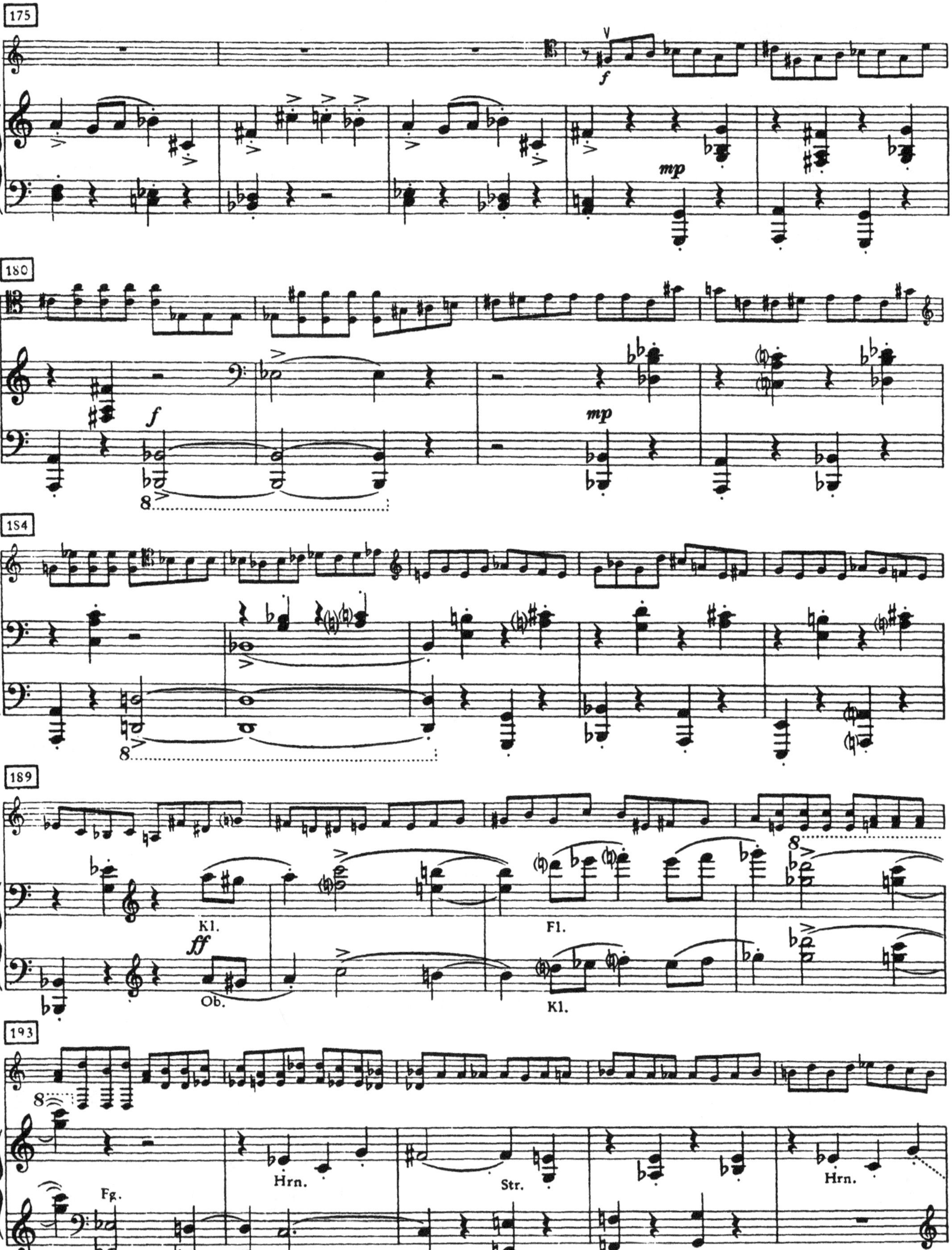
175
f
mp
180
f
mp
8
184
8
189
Kl.
Fl.
ff
Ob.
Kl.
8
193
8
Fg.
Hrn.
Str.
Hrn.
8

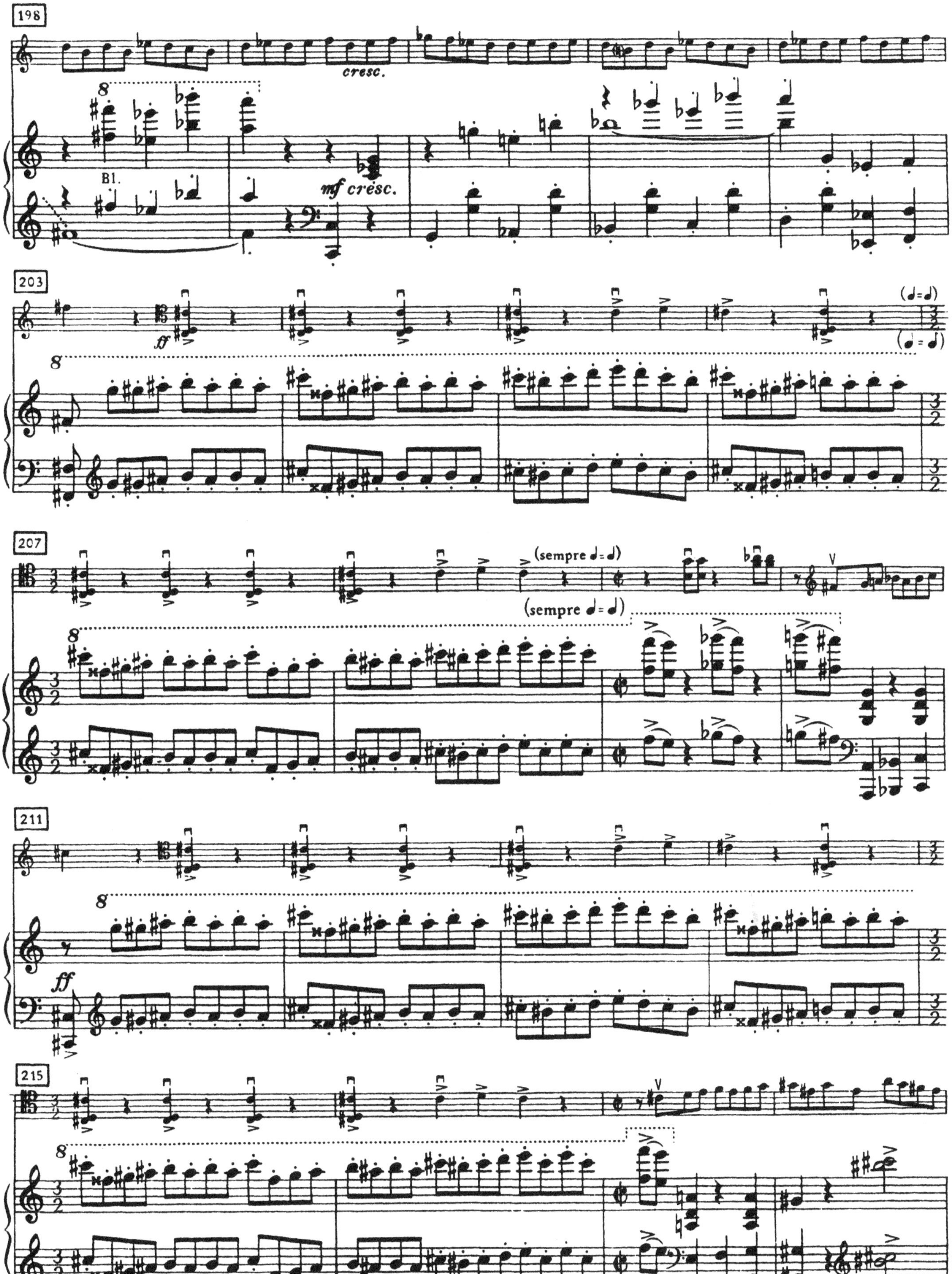
198
cresc.
8
Bl.
mf cresc.
203
ff
207
(sempre 𝅗𝅥 = ♩)
211
ff
215

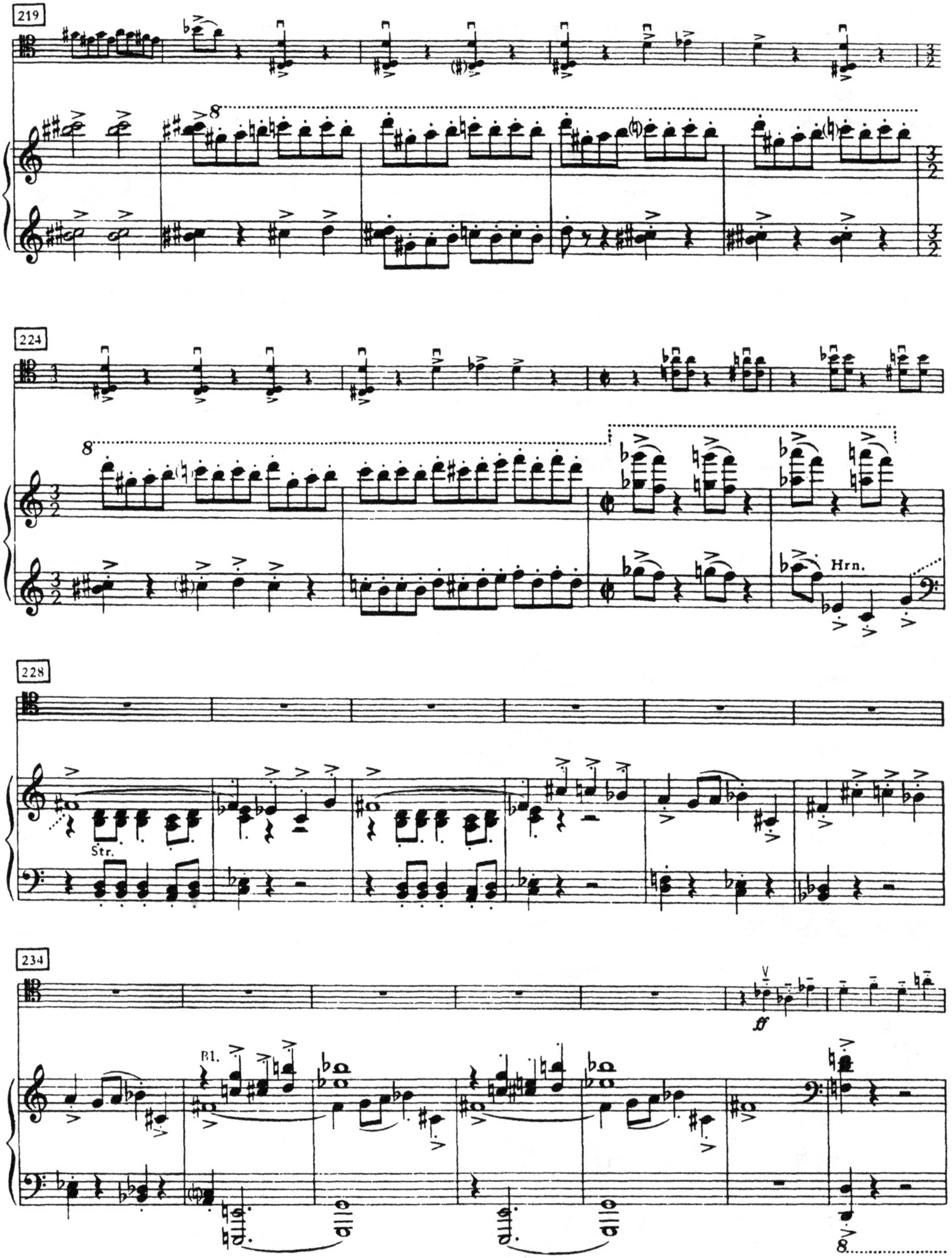
219
224
Hrn.
228
Str.
234
Bl.
ff

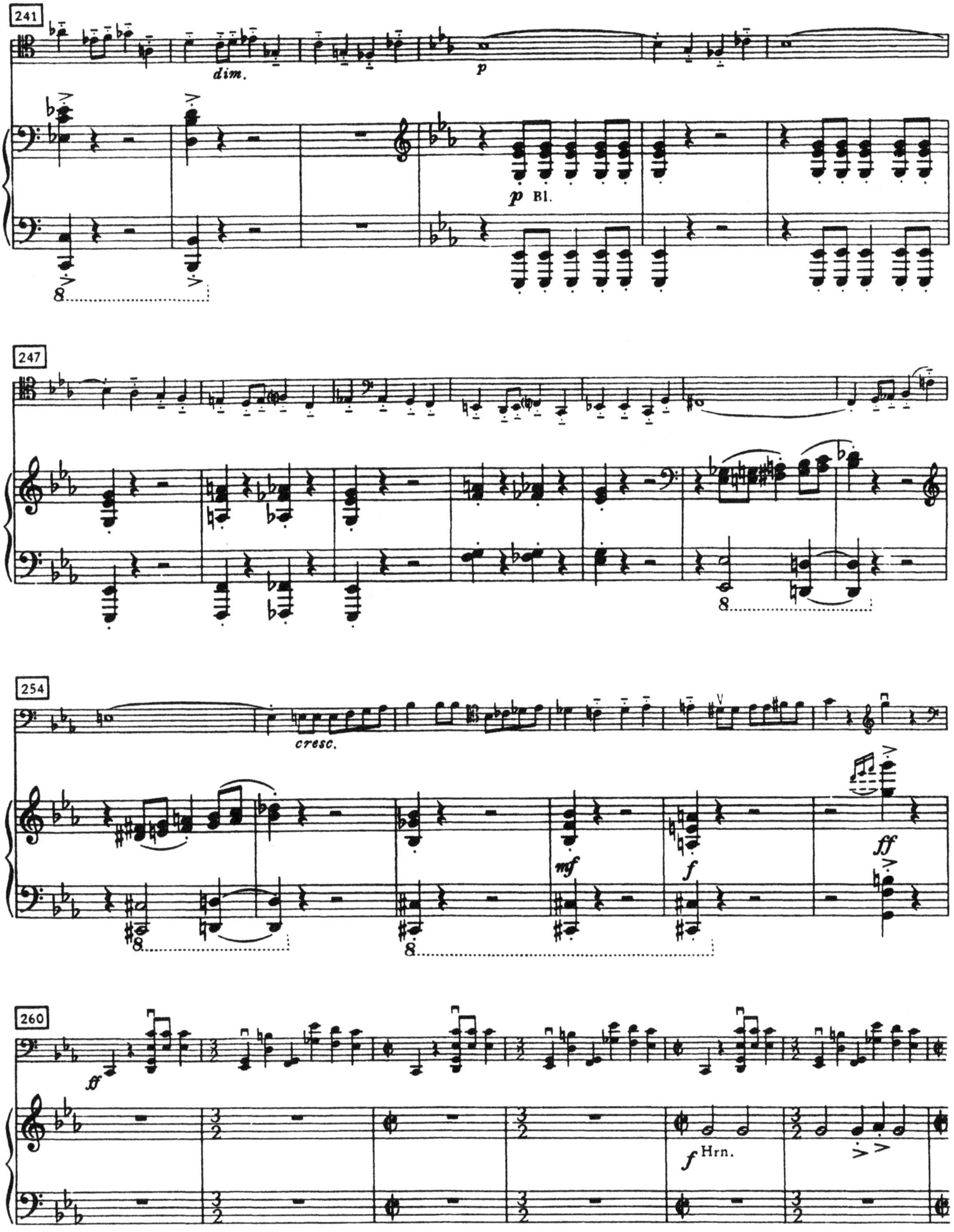
241
dim.
p
p Bl.
8
247
8
254
cresc.
mf
f
ff
8
260
ff
f Hrn.

14

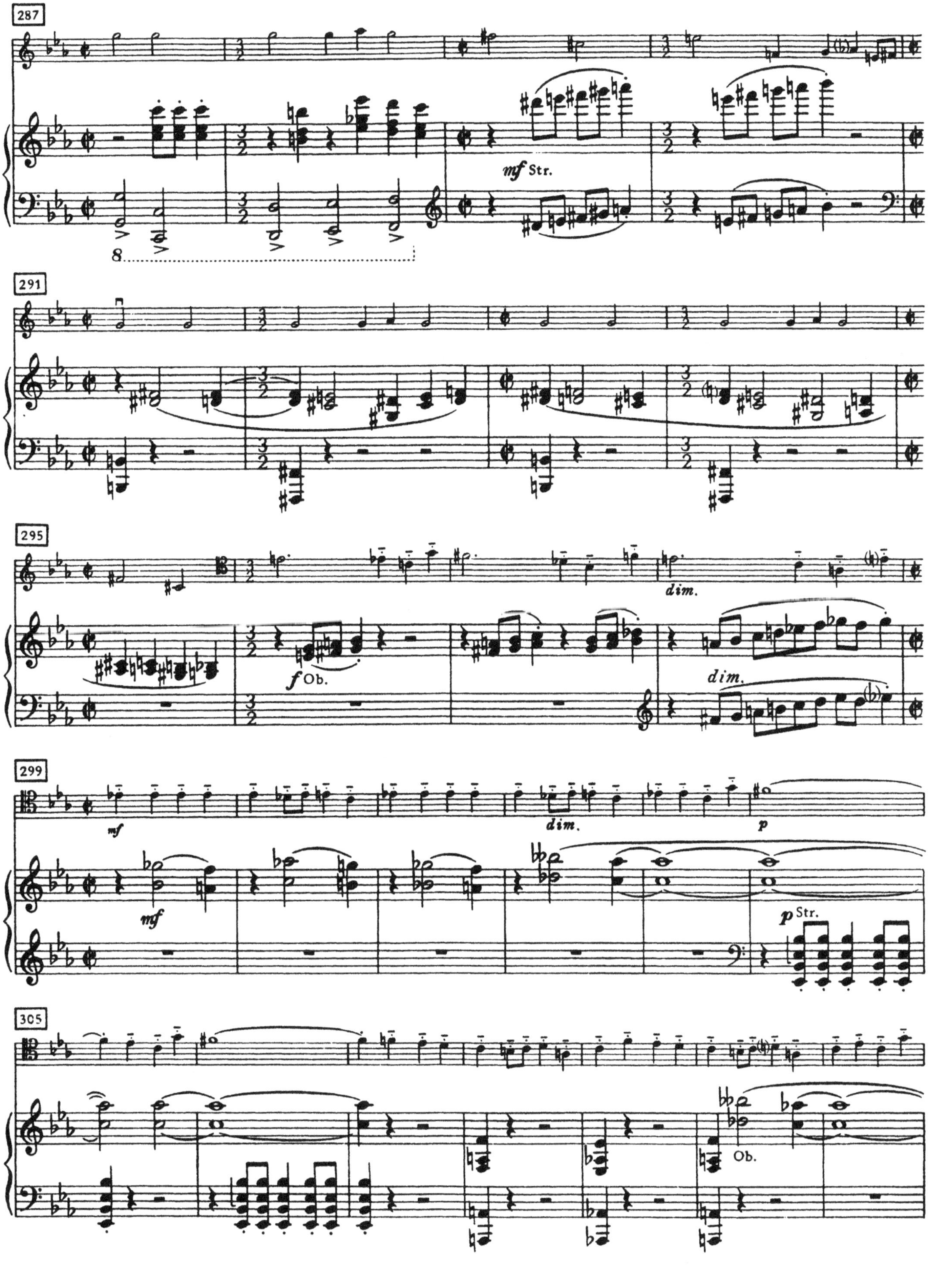
287
8
mf Str.
291
295
dim.
f Ob.
dim.
299
mf
mf
dim.
p
p Str.
305
Ob.

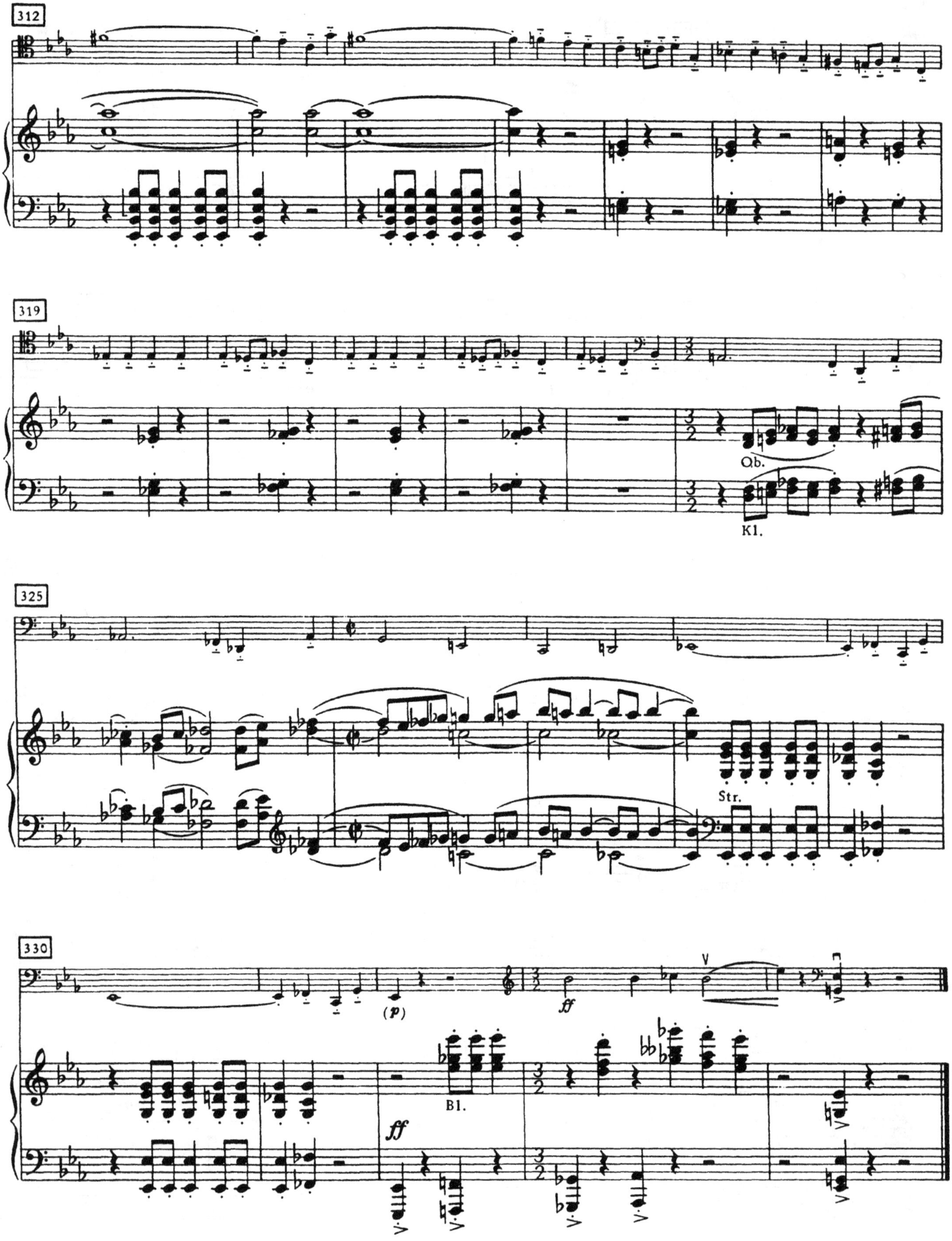
312
319
Ob.
Kl.
325
Str.
330
(p)
ff
ff
Bl.

II.

23
mf dim.
p
mp
28
32
cresc.
tenuto
mf
dim.
tenuto
p
Kl.
p espr.
36
cresc.
41
tenuto
mf
poco rit.
a tempo
pp subito
p
pp
Va.

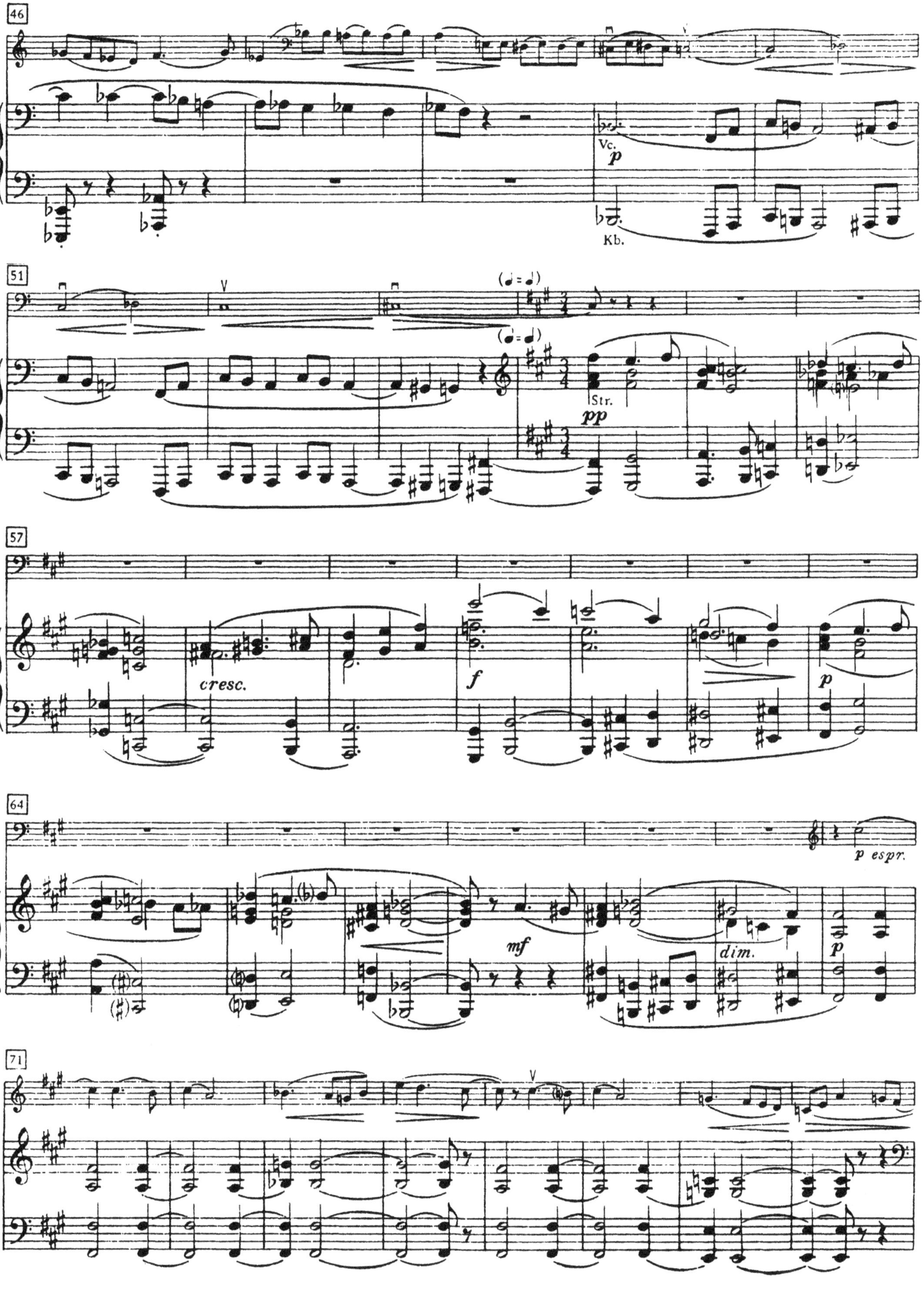
46
Vc.
p
Kb.
51
(♩ = ♩.)
(♩ = ♩.)
Str.
pp
57
cresc.
f
p
64
mf
dim.
p
p espr.
71

79
poco rit.
a tempo
cresc.
mf
dim.
p
poco rit.
a tempo
cresc.
mf dim.
p
86
pp
f
(♩=♩)
5/4
poco rit.
dim.
(♩=♩)
3/4
mf
92
a tempo
p
mf
rit.
a tempo
p
a tempo
rit.
a tempo
p
Bl.
p dolce, non stacc.
98
mf
(♩=♩)
5/4
poco rit.
dim.
(♩=♩)
3/4
mp
Str. (pizz.)

103
a tempo
p
(sempre 𝅗𝅥=𝅗𝅥)
a tempo
(sempre 𝅗𝅥=𝅗𝅥)
Bl.
dolce, non stacc.
Hrn.
108
Bl.
113
cresc.
f
cresc.
f
Str. (pizz.)
117
Bl.
f espr.

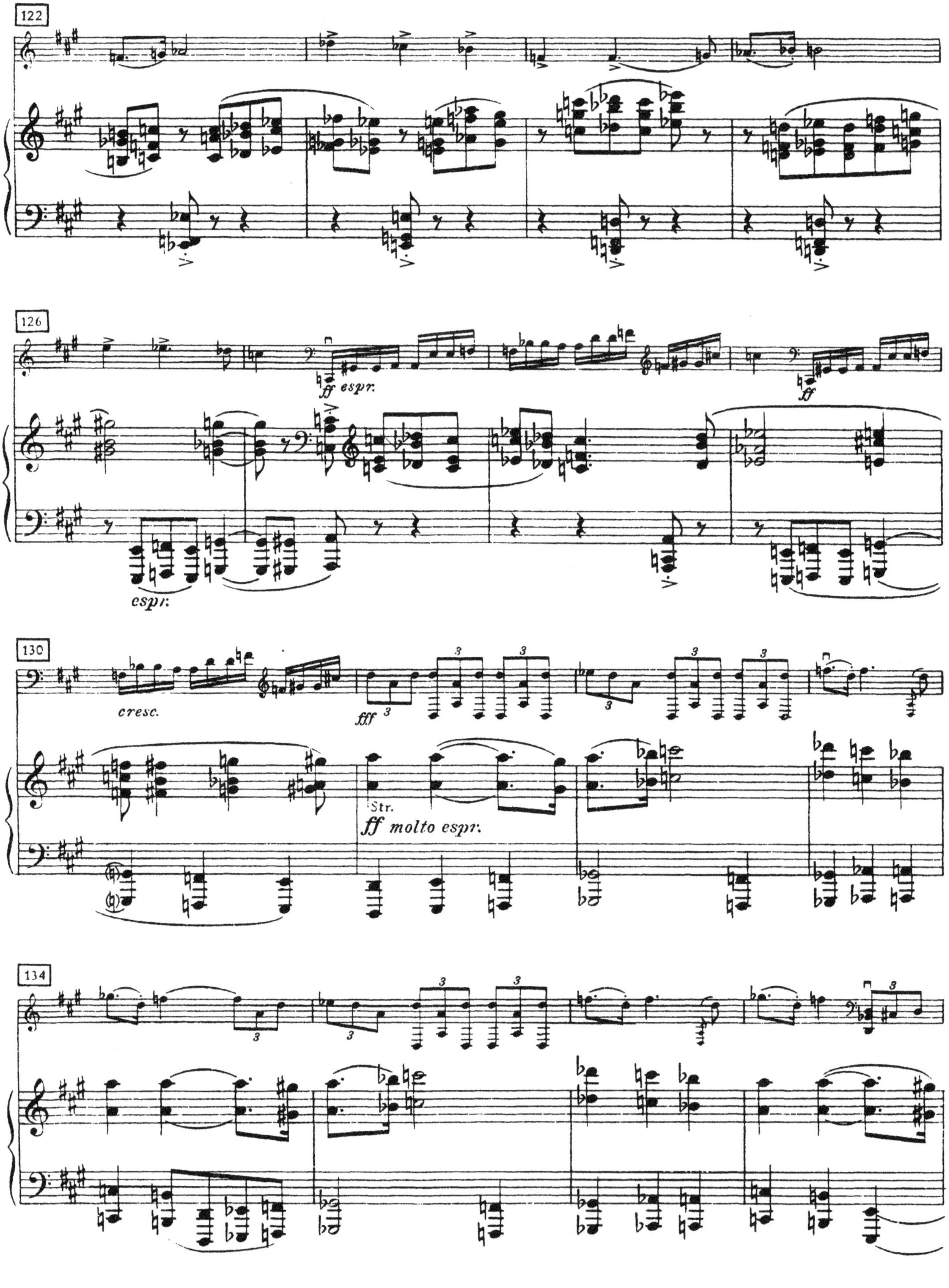
122
126
ff espr.
ff
espr.
130
cresc.
fff
Str.
ff molto espr.
134

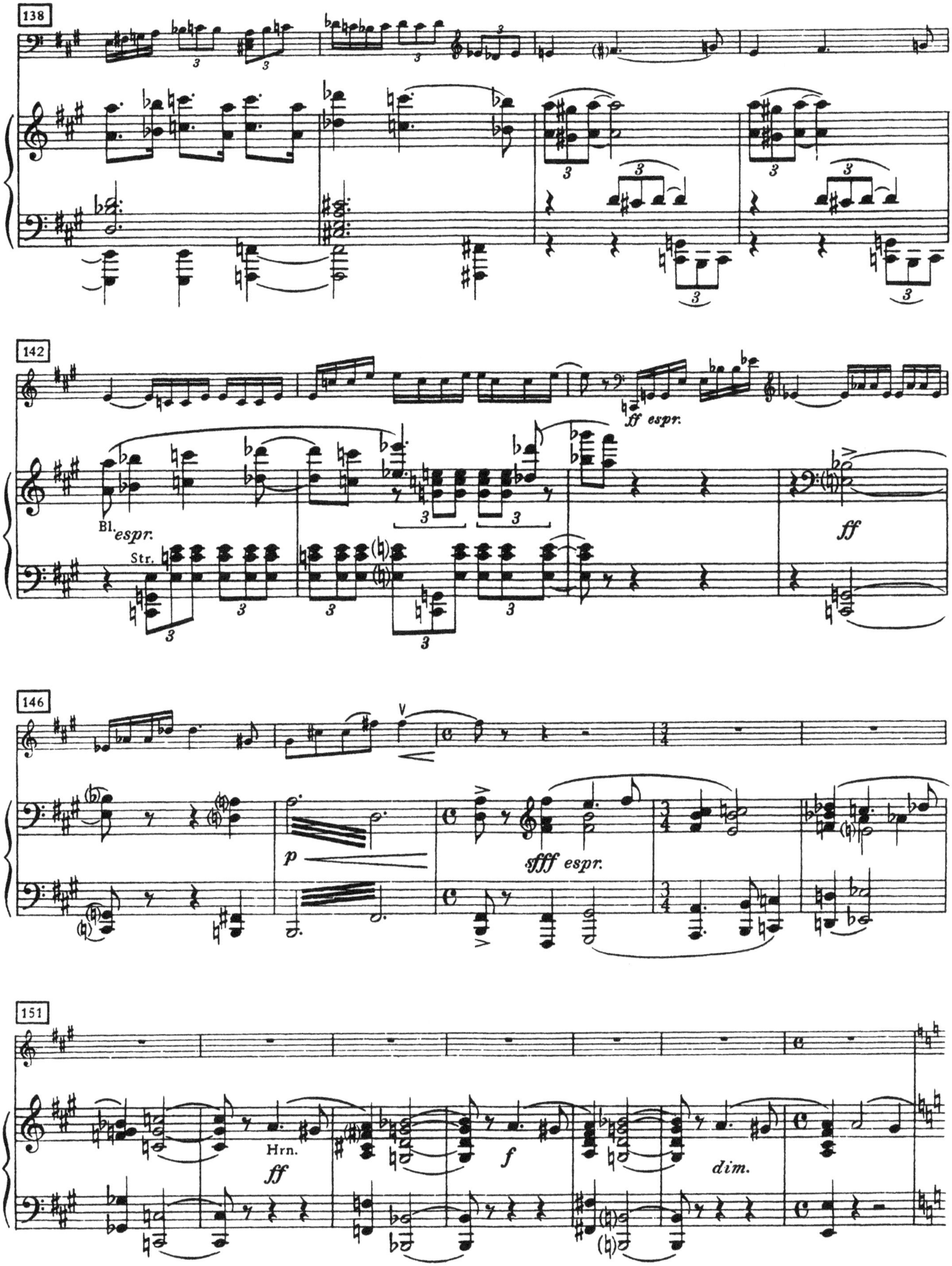
138
142
Bl.
espr.
Str.
ff espr.
ff
146
p
sfff espr.
151
Hrn.
ff
f
dim.

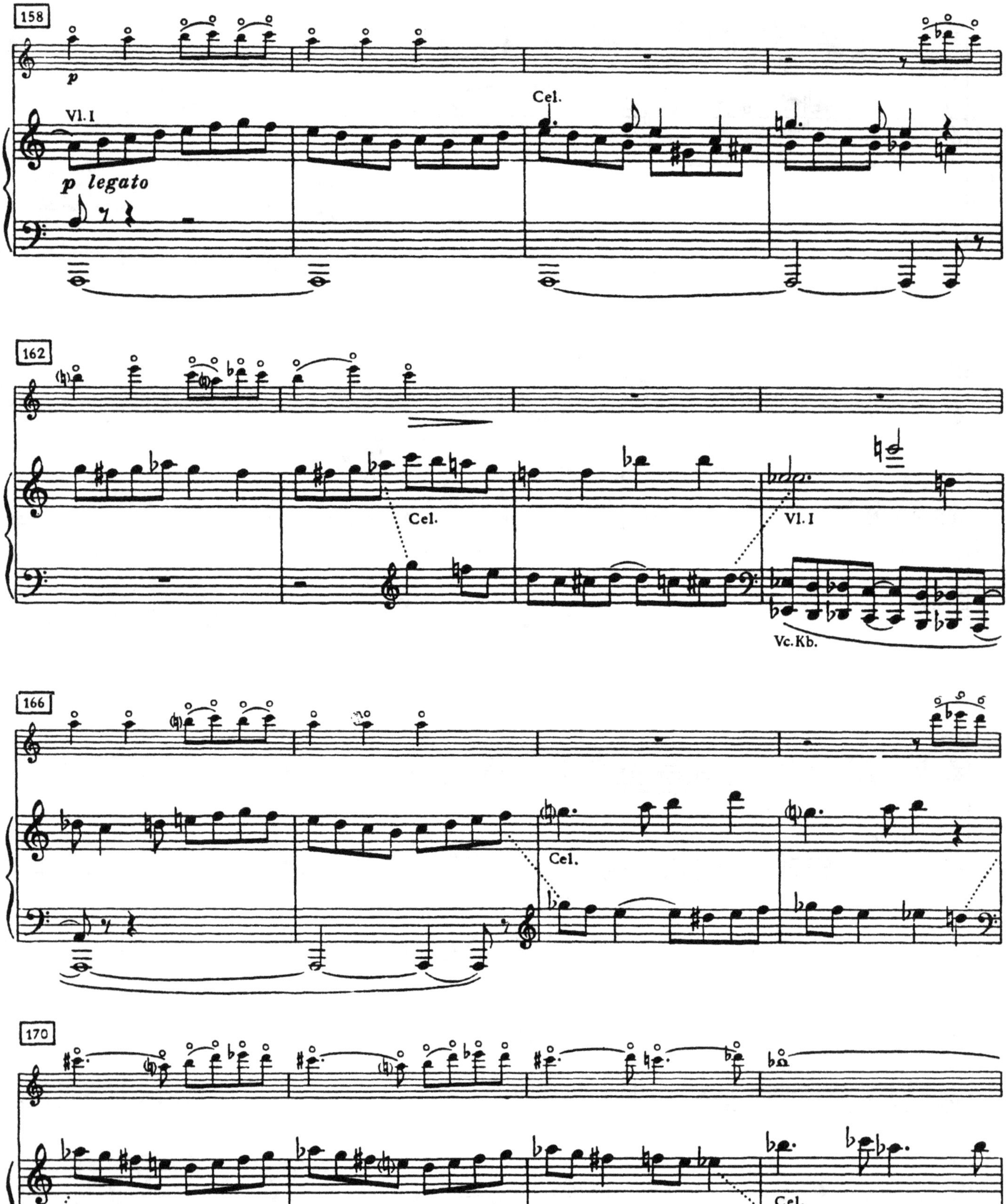
158
p
Vl. I
p legato
Cel.
162
Cel.
Vl. I
Vc. Kb.
166
Cel.
170
Cel.
Vl. I

174
Vl.II
8
178
Cel.
Kl.
8
Kl.
183
pp
Vc.Kb.
188
morendo
morendo
attacca

III.

CADENZA

pizz.
arco
p dim.
pizz.
(sempre
arco
cresc.
rit.
a tempo
dim.
cresc.
dim.
rit.
a tempo
pizz.
arco
accelerando poco a poco
cresc.
Allegretto

accelerando poco a poco
p cresc.
Allegro (♩= 144)
f
(♪= ♪)
(♪= ♪)
(sempre ♩= ♩)
Più mosso (♩= 160)
ff
attacca

IV.

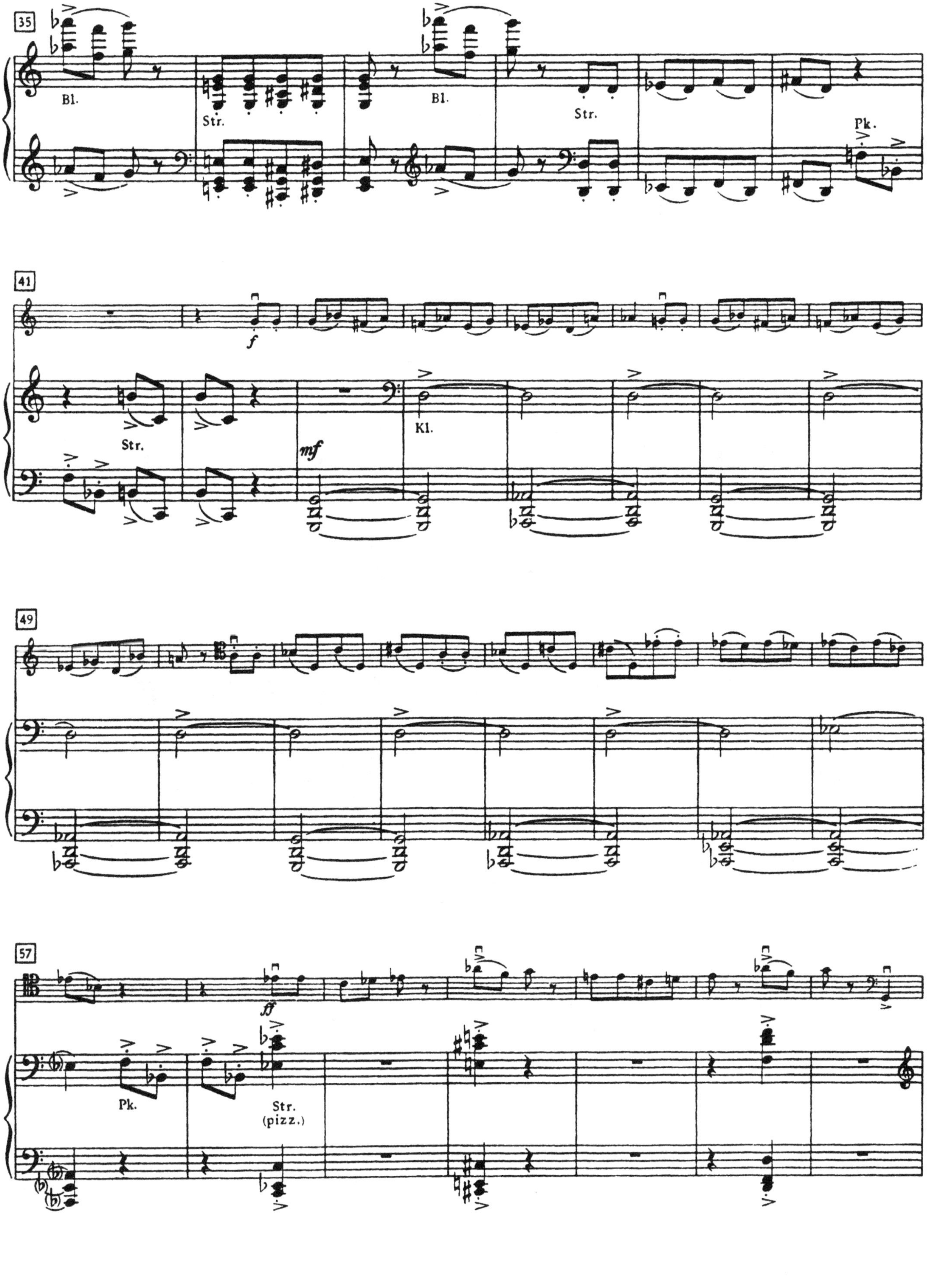
35
Bl.
Str.
Bl.
Str.
Pk.
41
f
Str.
mf
Kl.
49
57
ff
Pk.
Str.
(pizz.)

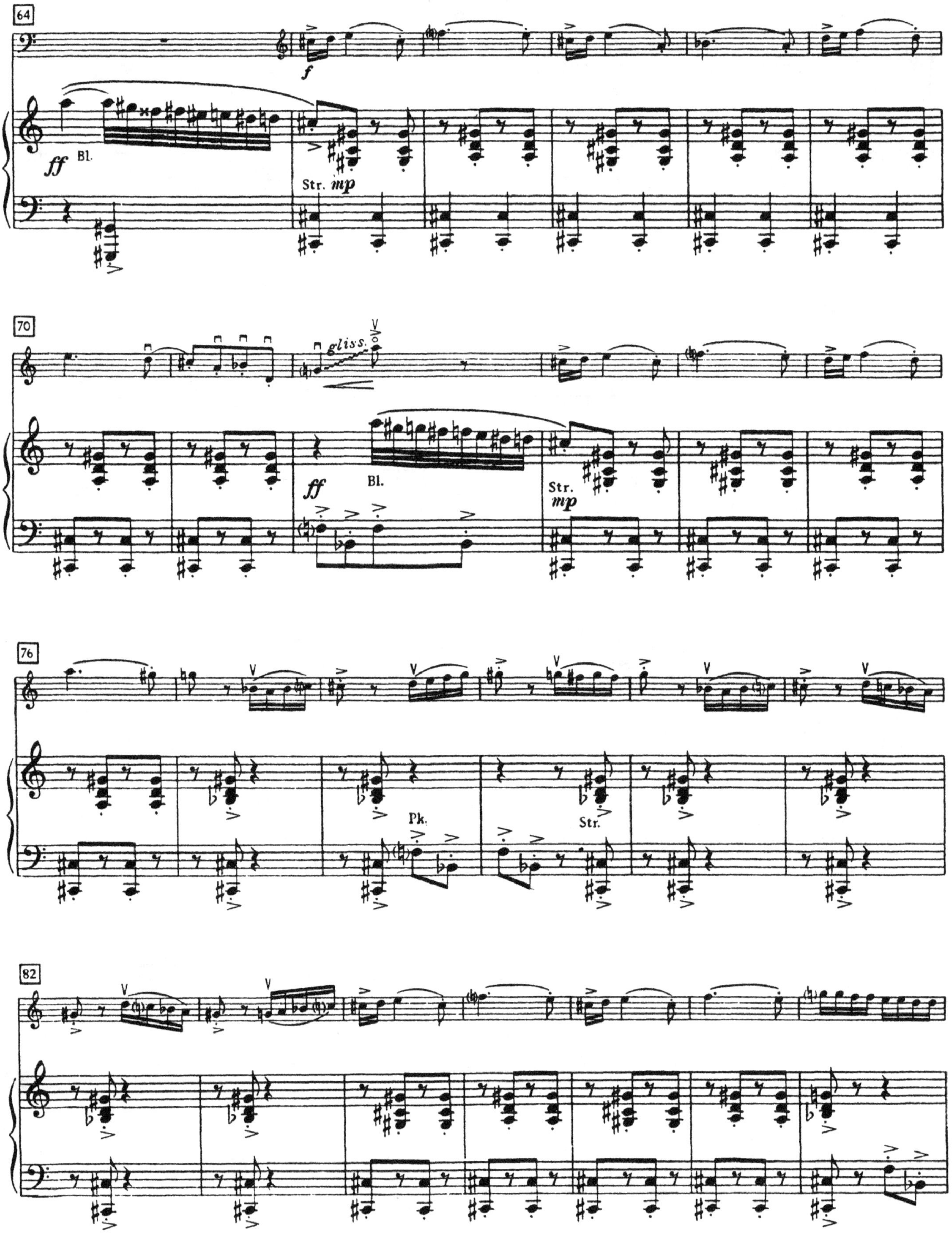
64
f
ff
Bl.
Str.
mp
70
gliss.
ff
Bl.
Str.
mp
76
Pk.
Str.
82

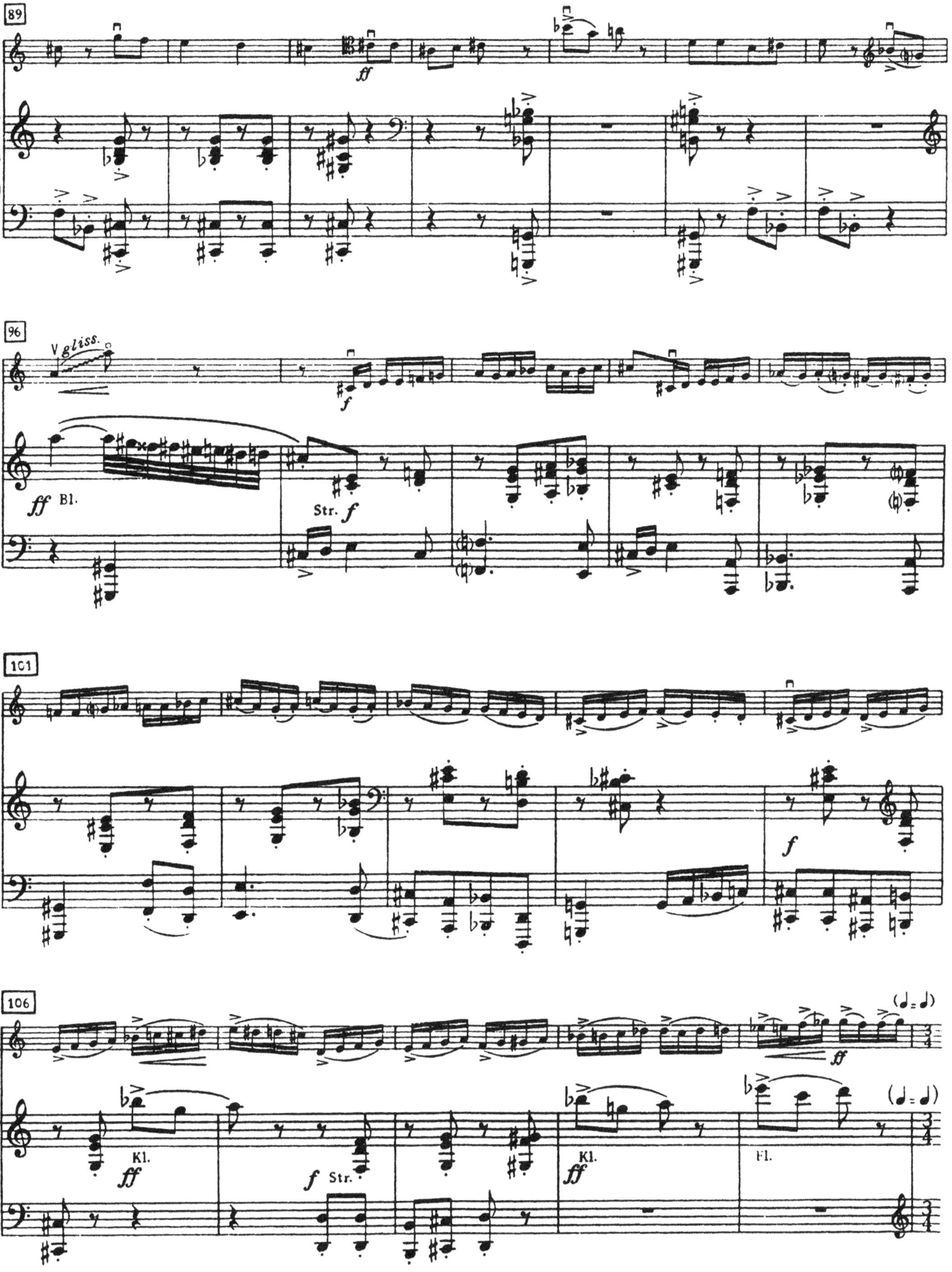
89
96
gliss.
Bl.
Str.
101
106
Kl.
Str.
Kl.
Fl.

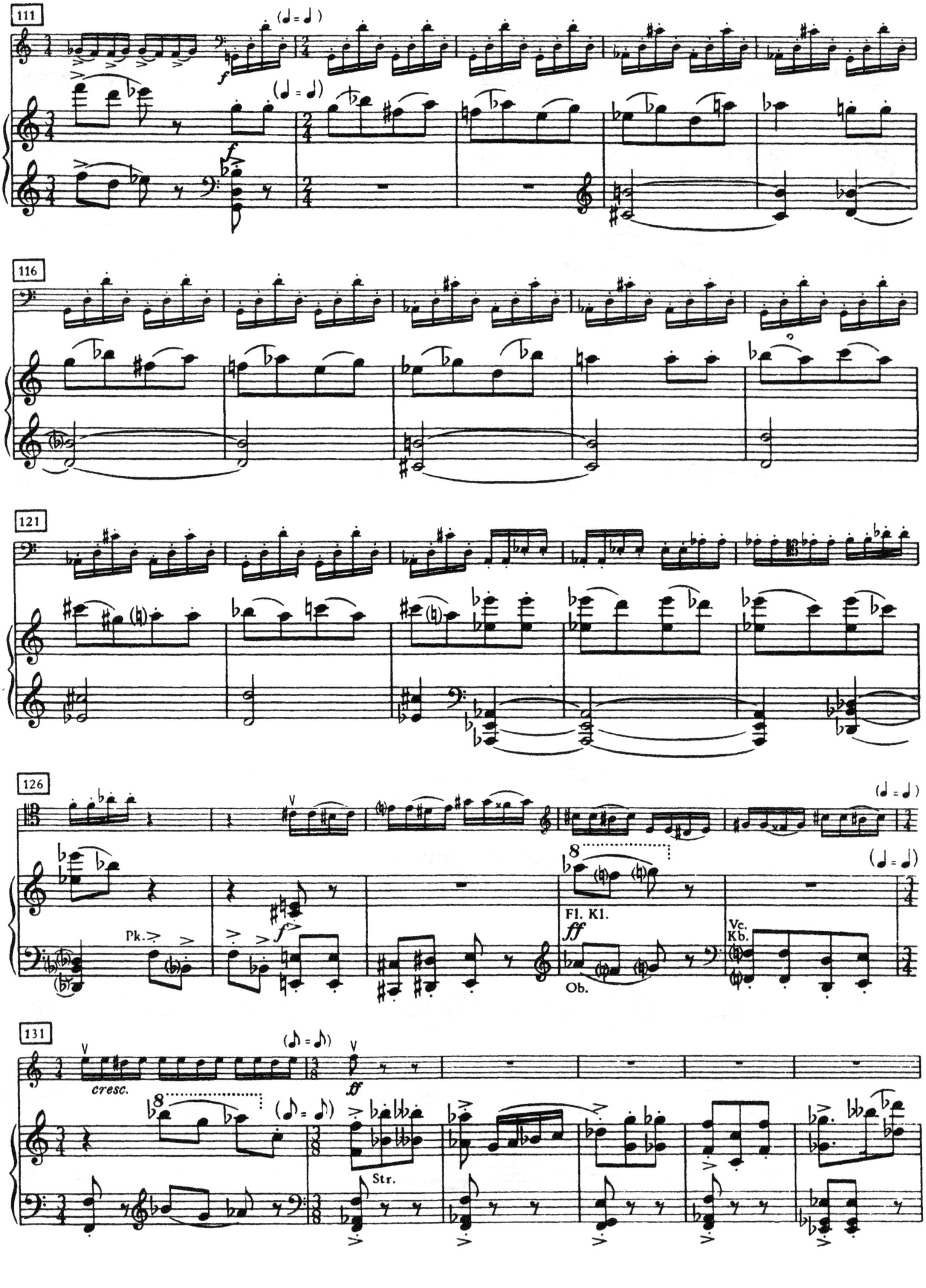
111
116
121
126
Pk.
Fl. Kl.
ff
Ob.
Vc.
Kb.
131
cresc.
ff
Str.

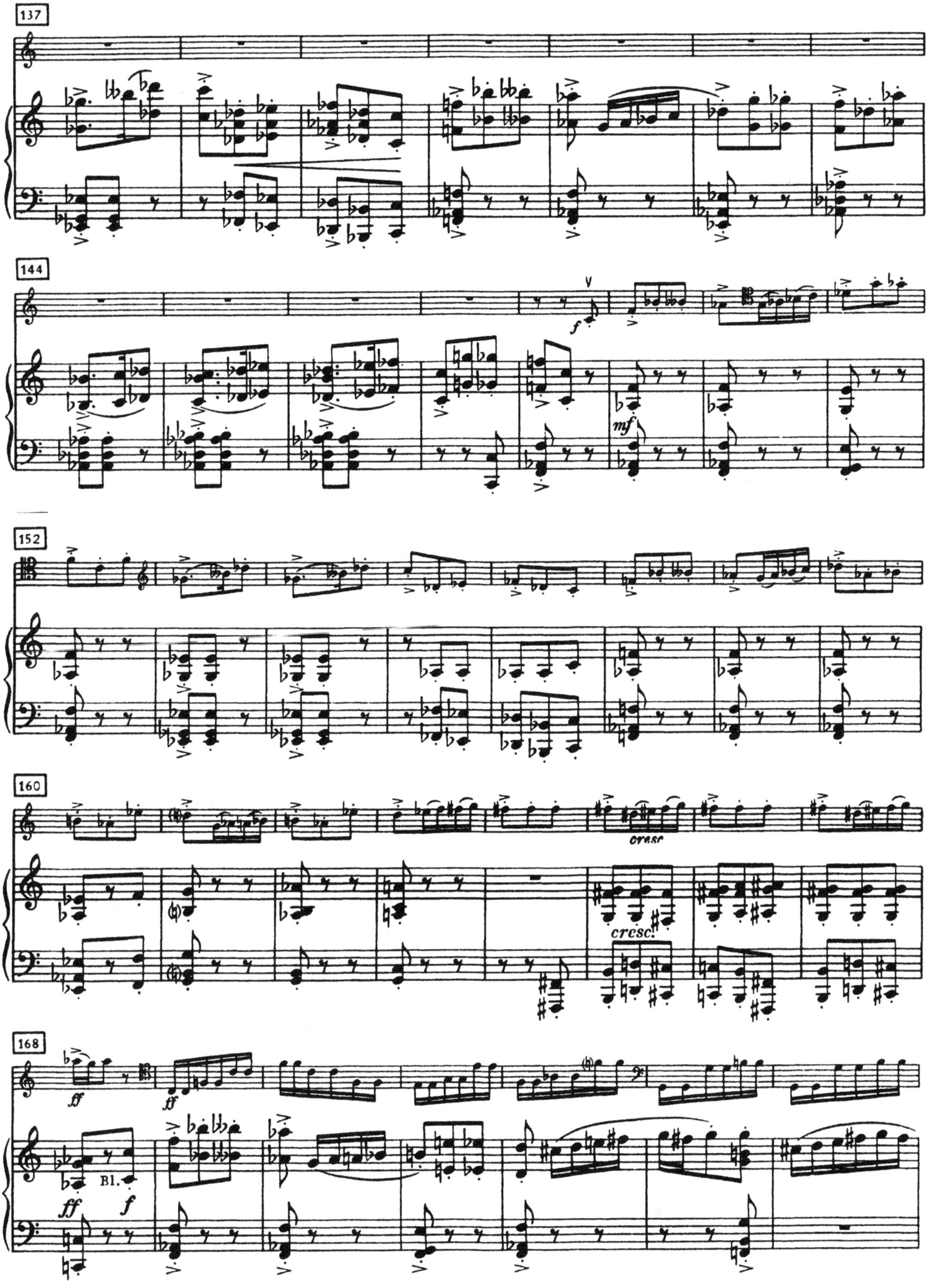
137
144
f
mf
152
160
cresc.
cresc.
168
ff
ff
Bl.
ff
f

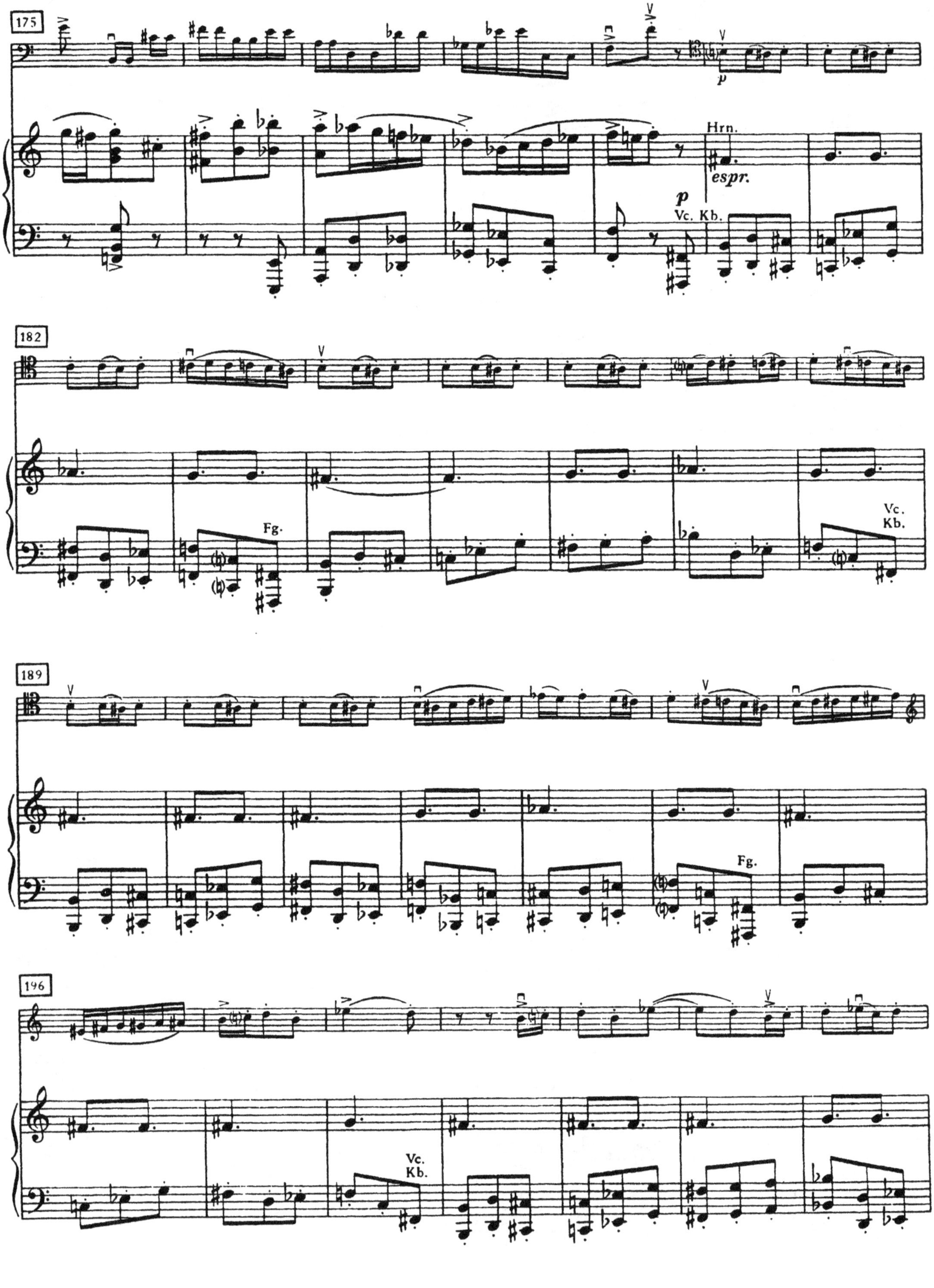
175
p
Hrn.
espr.
p
Vc. Kb.
182
Fg.
Vc.
Kb.
189
Fg.
196
Vc.
Kb.

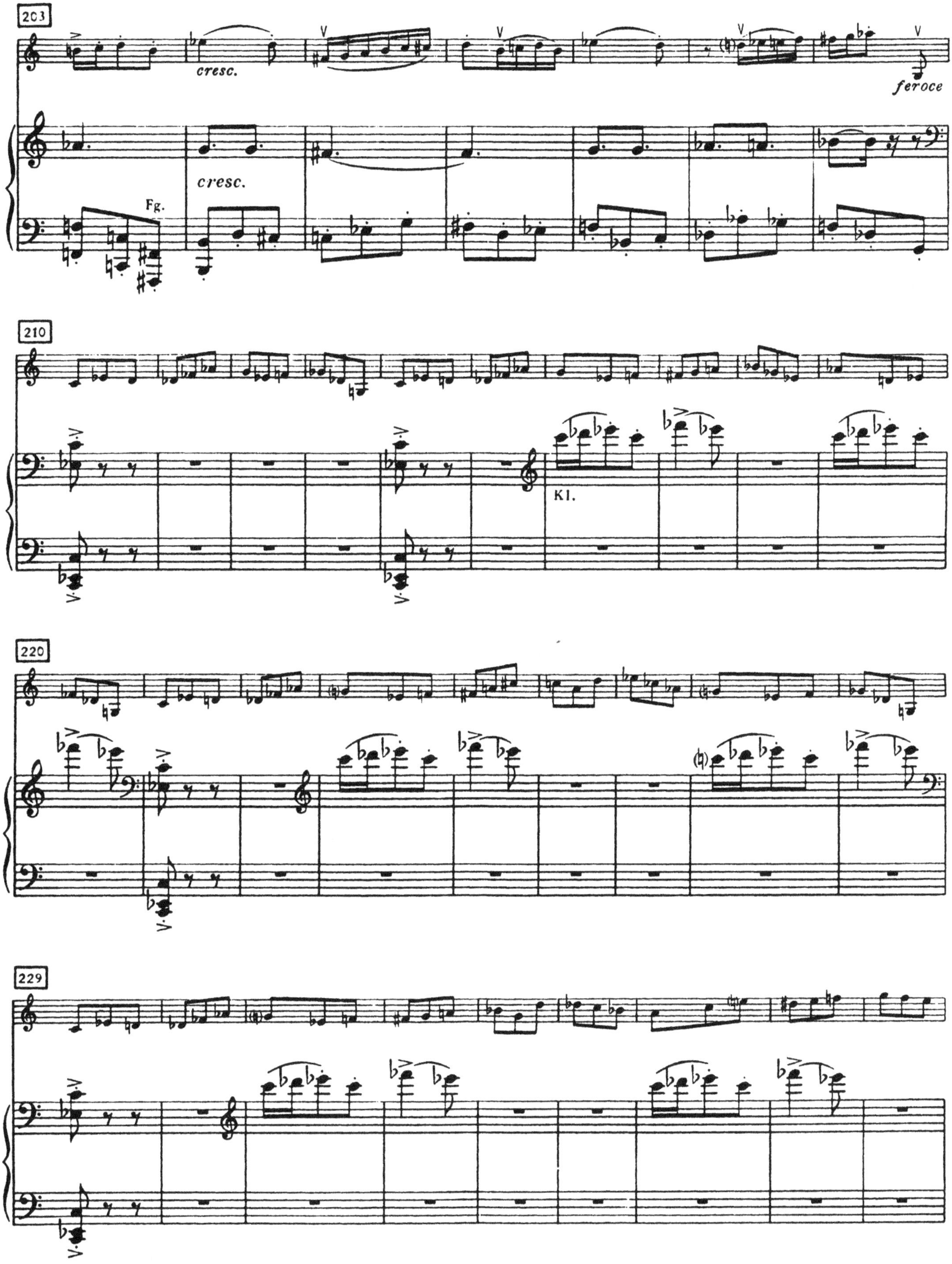
203
cresc.
feroce
cresc.
Fg.
210
Kl.
220
229

238
ff feroce
247
256
pizz.
ff
Bl.
265
Pk. ff
Bl. ff
273
arco
ff
ff
Str.
mf
Pk.
Bl. ff
Str.

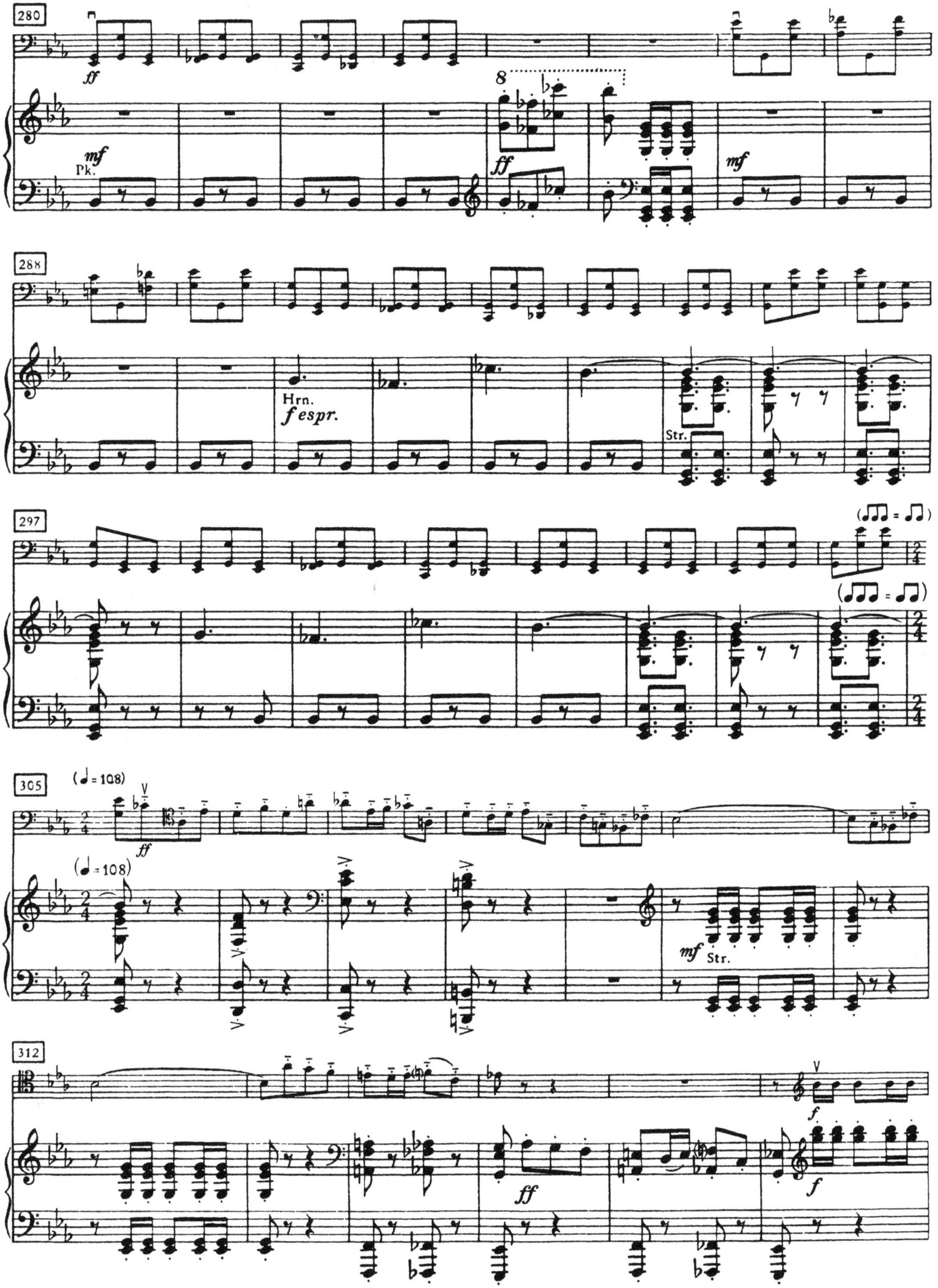
280
Pk.
Hrn.
f espr.
Str.
288
297
305
(♩ = 108)
312

38

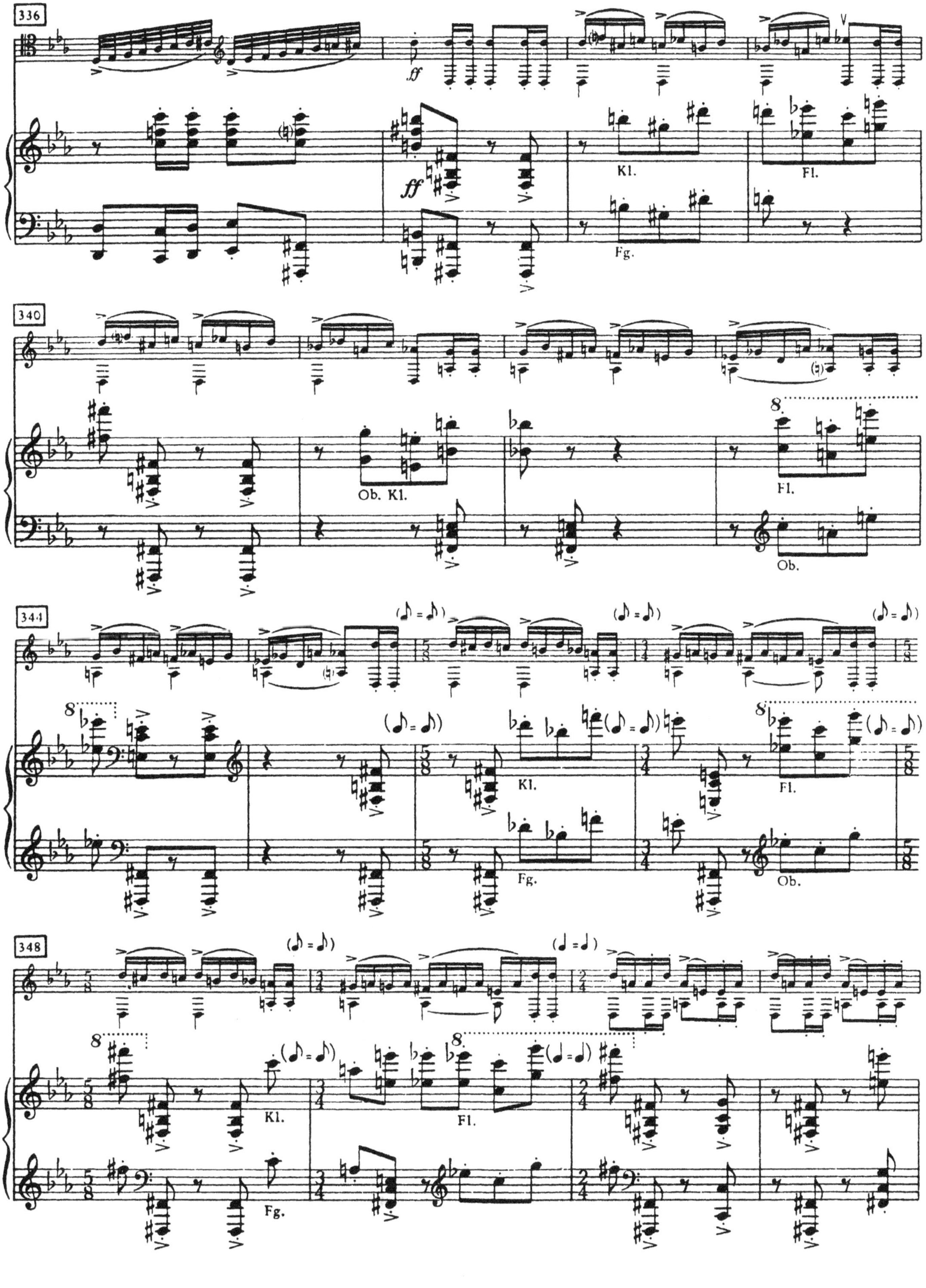
336
ff
ff
Kl.
Fl.
Fg.
340
8
Ob. Kl.
Fl.
Ob.
344
8
Kl.
Fl.
Fg.
Ob.
348
8
Kl.
Fg.
Fl.

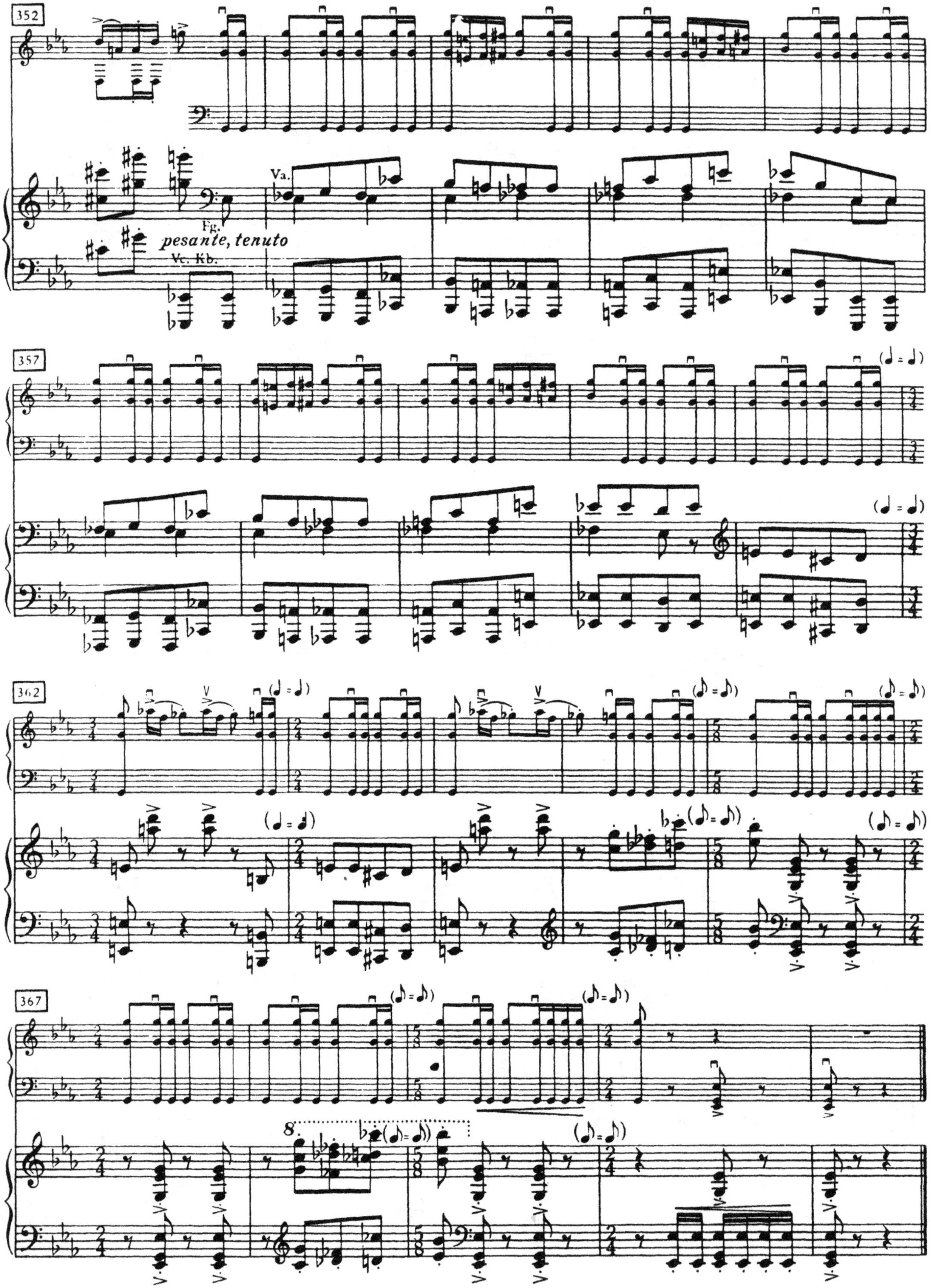
352
Va.
Fg.
pesante, tenuto
Vc. Kb.
357
362
367
8

www.ingramcontent.com/pod-product-compliance
Lightning Source LLC
Chambersburg PA
CBHW081242090426
42738CB00016B/3379